PRECARIOUS ROADS

TIARA

Made with ♥ on the Notion Press Platform
www.notionpress.com

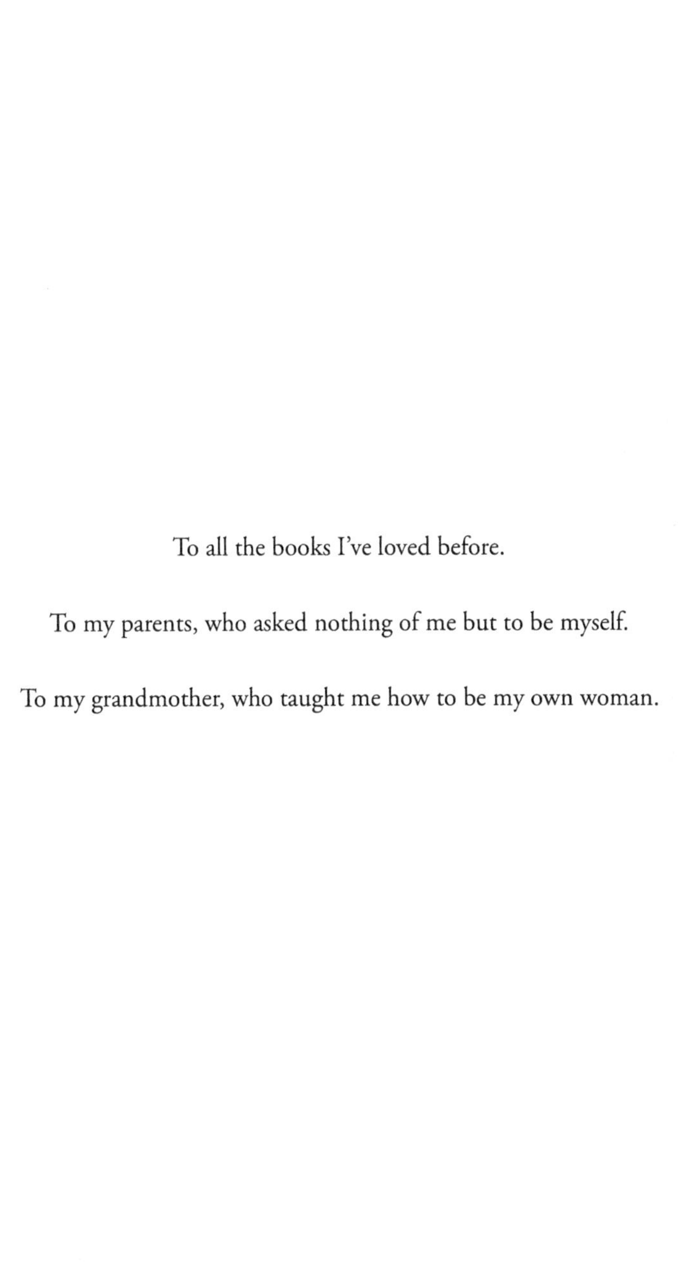

To all the books I've loved before.

To my parents, who asked nothing of me but to be myself.

To my grandmother, who taught me how to be my own woman.

Contents

Contents

Preface

I can't begin to express my gratitude to you dear reader for choosing this book.

Out of all beautifully illustrated, meticulously designed, and painstakinlgy written books standing upright on the shelf, you chose to read mine, nay, yours. For this heartbreaking set of poems is now yours. And yours only.

I started composing poems when I was a freshly exposed to the injustices of our world, finding the perfect anchor to my feelings through writing. I've always provided my grief and melancholia a safe haven in paper ever since.

This is my first book, and hopefully, there'll be many more to come. Stick with me, dear reader, and we'll make this memorable, I promise. And hey, I'm just a teenager trying to navigate my way through this labyrinth of emotions called life, so don't be too hard on me.

Signing off in awesomeness,

Tiara Arora.

Acknowledgements

I would first and foremost, express unending gratitude to my parents. If they hadn't introduced me to the world of literature, I would never have gone astray and found my true self in the wilderness. Indeed, thank you for setting me up with the greats that i started off with- Enid Blyton and J.K. Rowling.

A special note of thanks to all my English teachers, including my mom, for making me read and summarize classics, like Black Beauty and Macbeth. Without you, I probably would never have buried my head in dusty old bookshelves in an era of brand-new iPhones and home-theatres.

Had I been lucky at being 'Miss-popular' through my initial years of school, I would never have fallen in love with the smell of the pages of a novel. So, yes, I thank my bullies, 'friends' and the boys who never treated me right, for letting me find solace among high-ceilinged and wooden-floored libraries while I had from the hellish tatteredness of life.

I also credit all the people that have rooted for me, even if for a second. My persistant relatives, who asked me to never give up on my will to write. My excellent friends, who pushed me to channel my inner magnificence all the damn time. Myself, of course, for if I had given into the misery of daily routine, I would never have mustered the courage to give this my all. And last but not the least, my dearest readers, because without you, my dream would have always been just a dream.

I am eternally fortunate for you all.

Chapter1

I travelled precarious roads,
Ones with no end,
But all closed doors.
I walked, and I walked,
To miles afar,
Until I found one of them ajar.
But alas!
It wasn't the door I desired,

For your love had been encased in glass.
I travelled precarious roads,
Winding deeper into your heart,
But never found what I was looking for,
Yes, it was the past,
And your love had been encased in glass.
I travelled precarious roads,
Ones with no end,
But all closed doors.
I walked, and I walked,
To miles afar,
Until I found one of them ajar.
But alas!
It wasn't the door I desired,
For your love had been encased in glass.
I travelled precarious roads,
Winding deeper into your heart,
But never found what I was looking for,
Yes, it was the past,
And your love had been encased in glass.
I travelled precarious roads,
Ones with no end,
But all closed doors.
I walked, and I walked,
To miles afar,
Until I found one of them ajar.
But alas!

It wasn't the door I desired,
For your love had been encased in glass.
I travelled precarious roads,
Winding deeper into your heart,
But never found what I was looking for,
Yes, it was the past,
And your love had been encased in glass.

Chapter2

When you came,

The sun did not start shining.

It dimmed,

And the days faded away to dusk.

Chapter3

you want me,
to look at you
like the moon
looks at the sun.
"how can i?", i say,
"when its the other way round?

when you are my moon,
my only pitch of light
in the echoing darkness?"

Chapter6

I think it's funny,
How only the thought of your arms
Wrapped around me
Puts me to sleep

Chapter7

You are a world of your own.
You are an entity in yourself.
An entity, a world for which
My feelings will be as permanent as possible.

Chapter8

I wish I could stare at you forever
Your beauty speaks to me
On levels I can't explain,

It enchants me- perhaps you were
So artfully created
By God- she is so clever
I wish I could stare at you forever
I dream that the universe conspires
To hold me captivated….
It pauses when I look at you-
The birds stop chirping, the stars stop shooting
Nothing but my eyes are moving
As I search your face,
I don't want to stop- hoping never, never
I wish I could stare at you forever.

Chapter9

those who fall in love
are tricked.
lucky me, for i have
fallen in the deep
vast, oblivious ocean
with the stormiest waves,

that is you.

Chapter10

when you said
you loved me
my whole world
came to a standstill.
when you said
you love me
i gave you
all my empty spaces
all you could fill.

Chapter11

Life stopped changing.

I sat there,

Hoping, praying, wishing

It would stay that way forever.

Chapter12

Walking through hell for you,
These fires don't burn me anymore.
Fighting my demons for you,
Their echoes don't scare me anymore.
Love, I'll brave all dangers for you,
This dark world can't defeat me anymore,
This dark world can't break me anymore.

Chapter13

Every time I think of you and I,
It's like I plummet myself another ten feet,
Down into a bottomless abyss.

But oh, how I wish you would fall along,
Fall with me,
Deep into the love I miss.

Chapter14

if you are happily mine,
can you love me for my cries?
even when i only shine,
can you love me for my dark skies?

Chapter15

Is this how it ends?
My heart broken by unfastening threads,
Trying to make amends,
Is this how it ends?

Chapter16

When you left,

The sun dipped further on……

Chapter17

how does it feel?
not being mine,
deserting my dark skies,
to be someone else's sunshine?

Chapter18

I look at you and i see,
the way you look at me
isn't the same
as it used to be.
i look at you and i see,
the dreams we used to share
aren't mine anymore,
but hers to dream.
i look at you and i see,
how easy it was for you
to break my heart,
and walk right out on me.

i look at you and i see,
the way you look at me,
isn't the same
as it used to be.

Chapter19

I feel so complicated,
Over-chaotic and lost
Often, it hits me
That I could just give up,
But at what cost?
You were everything to me,
All my highs and lows.
But now I look at the garden of our love,
And watch how in place of each rose,
A pricking thorn grows.
While I still naming each star,

Slowly, our sky became a blur.
And I went on too far
While you had already,
Built another universe with her.
It's this impact you have on me,
Where everything starts falling apart
And the world seldom makes sense anymore.
When I think of you,
From my dark ocean of feelings,
Nothing washes up ashore.
I feel so messed up and lost,
Over – dramatic and lost,
Often, it hits me
That I could just give up,
But at what cost?

Chapter20

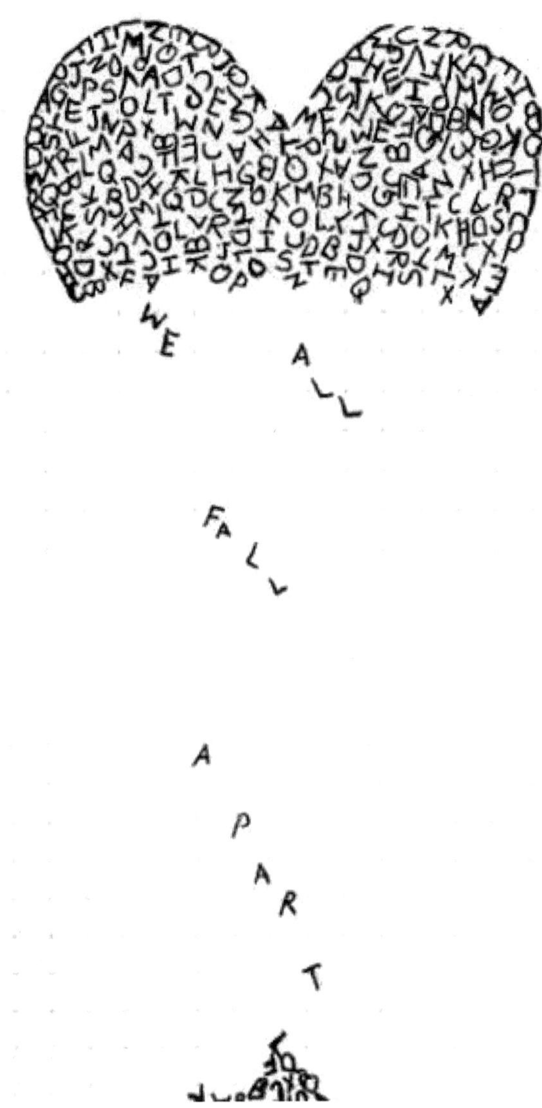
WE
ALL
FALL
APART

The melancholy dawns upon you,
Telling you,
That love is a lot more,
Than just hugs and kisses.
It is something you feel,
You experience,
You cry for, and
Fight the whole world for.
And if it is even a bit less than that,
It isn't love.

Chapter21

Chapter22

I'm drowning in despair,
My life now beyond repair.
A voice in me longs to shout out,
Driven away by sorrow and doubt.
Can you see me in the dim light,
Struggling to come back in sight?

Chapter23

He asks me, how I've been holding up.
His voice sends me far away.
I picture myself,
Eating only to survive,
Smiling wide enough to sustain,
Sleeping as if it were a dive, and
Walking away enough to abstain

From the loose ends of hope that
Perhaps, still remain.
Hey! He asks me again.
His voice brings me back,
To the place where,
I break out of my reverie,
Going about with reality,
Burying these flashes
Of the sad, broken me.

Chapter24

I lie down with our memories
In the middle of the night,
Dreaming of what we were supposed to be.
Thinking of how I would have changed it
If I had it in me.
One thing leads to another,
And everything leads to you in my mind.
I hope, pray and wish
For a love that was right,
When I lie down on our memories
In the middle of the night.
Often, it's just my feelings eating me up,
And you are almost out of my head,
But then the ghosts zoom into sight
Reminding me why
I'm lying down with our memories
In the middle of the night.
The bed feels so cold and unfamiliar,
The room so empty, so devoid of light
And it all comes down to my demons,
Those you ran away from,
And those I constantly need to fight,

As I lie down on our memories,
In the middle of the night.
Oh love, I lie down on our memories,
In the middle of the night.
Dreaming of what we could we have been,
Wondering whether I would do it right,
If I had it in me.

Chapter25

I sit and watch you,
Ruin everything we've had
Guessing it was a different picture
In your head that you drew.
So, does it end here,
You, blaming me of the smallest errors
When the whole world did
The same to you, my dear?
I suppose you do not give me much to say,
For I fear joining you in the dark,
Praying to soon see the light of day.
And when this is all done,
I imagine I would remember
All the signs burning bright,
But how could I have left you and run?
Alright then, leave me here to cry,
As I sit and watch you
Stomping over the roses in our garden,
Abandoning them to die.

Chapter26

It's a summer eve.
The heat would have killed me,
But it doesn't.
My head spins with misery
Wondering how I ended up feeling
So lonely,
So empty.
It's a summer eve.
The skies never turn dark here,
Although, they are never bright either,
At least not in my heart,
Not in the place where I still hold you near.
It's a summer eve.
The sun shines its rays,
And it takes me back,
Back to that winter day
When you held my hand, my soul
Soothing me over, saying, you'll love me always.
It's a summer eve.
The streets lay vacant day and night,
Shattering my hopes of seeing you,
Once again.

I know you don't come here
Anymore,
But I pray, that you just might.
It's a summer eve.
Oh, what a brilliant summer eve,
It would have been,
If you wouldn't have lost
"interest" (as if I were an object)
That you decided to, just
Leave.

Chapter27

It's been a week now
They haven't bothered to check
On how I'm doing and where I've been
And they don't care if I'm a wreck.
So lost in their upper-world circles
Discussing who they kissed on the neck
During their fancy weekend parties
And how they want to bedeck
Their lives with self-love and care.
When it's two in the night, I hear a voice
And my anxiety says to me,
"If they were true to you,
They'd never let you be."
And like a fever dream, it feels picturesque:
All my relations coming undone,
Perhaps I never even needed them: it's perfect.
I zone back in, and it's been some time now,
They haven't bothered to check
On how I've been keeping up with my demons
'coz they don't even care if I'm a wreck.
And these are the same folks I've called
Time and again my friends....

Chapter29

Only, this time,

The nights gave way

to a new dawn.

Chapter30

You put me on a pedestal,
As if it was never hard for me.
As if from my own mind,
I didn't want to flee.
As if it was all so easy.
Believe me,
If there was anything I could,
I would do, for you to just see.

Chapter31

the worst feeling is when
you wanna cry,
but your tears
are scared of the outside world.
the worst feeling is when
you wanna say something
with your heart and soul,
but your mind doesn't
allow them to.
the worst feeling is when
you realize burnt matches
don't light up again.

Chapter32

You abandoned my heart and soul,
I guess I meant little to you.

But I found my way through the dark,
To the sunshine as I always do.
And beware of the cruelties,
'coz this time,
It's going to be someone new.

Chapter33

You go round and round,
Wandering the city.
Everyone thinks you're
So wild, so cool, so free.
Not me, though.
I know you.
I know your reality.
You have been places,
In search for the one thing
That you could only ever find in me.

Chapter34

Love is a void,
That will always remain unfulfilled,
Until you start loving yourself.

Chapter35

My mind is a
Dangerous place
To be.
But I'd rather be here,
Than with you.

Chapter36

I saw your city from the hill,
It was calling out to me,
Pulling across the lakes and farms,
Sprawling below majestically,
Right into your arms.
The lush green hues of your life,
Reminded me of the transient times we spent,
And the shallow promises we made for love.
How foolish I was, when I thought you were the one

God had sent for me, from the heavens above.
Oh, the lush green hues of life,
Gave me a nostalgic serendipity,
Something I never thought I would find,
When I saw your city.
The loneliness that wound down the hair-pin roads,
Strangling me inside and out
Trapping me with its iron chains,
Seemed to fade away with the mist.
But a voice in me still yearned to shout out,
Our lost tale of joys and pains,
Telling the world about a portrait
Of love, that once was as pretty,
As the sight from the hill,
When I saw your city.
The bright blue airspaces
Shrouding the landscape all over,
Were as empty, weight less and yet,
As heavy, as the thoughts,
That never ceased to hover,
About how we ended up in such a mess.
Our ancient, reminisced love,
Remained nothing but a forgotten pity,
Dissolving in the sky
As quick as it flew in,
When I saw your city.
Walking back from the hill,

I felt the knots loosen in me,
Thinking of how,
Even across the lakes and farms,
Sprawling below majestically
Your distant love
Was pulling me right into your arms,
When I saw your city.

Chapter37

I travelled precarious roads,
Seeming never-ending.

But then,
Came a slight bending,
Leading me to sun-lit meadows,
Where the river of new life flows.
I sat there,
spending months with myself,
embracing the new me,
and to all the screaming voices,
growing deaf.
The spirit of joy, one day
From the river arose,
Guiding me all through the meadows,
That wouldn't have been mine,
If I hadn't travelled those precarious roads.

Printed by Libri Plureos GmbH in Hamburg, Germany